Jessie's Story

hearts.

ure

Jessie's Story

The Inspiration and Life Behind Jessie's Fund

Sharon Stinson

HABITANSIA PRESS
Watsonville, California

Jessie's Story: The Inspiration and Life Behind Jessie's Fund

Published by:

HABITANSIA PRESS
P.O. Box 1986
Watsonville, CA 95076

www.habitansia.com

Book and cover design: Karyn Wolf Lynn

Printed simultaneously in the United Kingdom and the United States of America.

ISBN 0-9774837-0-3

These stories are dedicated to Hannah, who came before Jessie, and to Jacob, who followed after.

Jessica George

Photo by Lucy Russell

Table of
CONTENTS

The Evening Sun

I was walking along the beach,
I saw the evening sunlight
It was really so very bright
The sun was orange and yellow

Whilst I heard the wind's big bellow
The sun was twinkling on the sea
How nice and beautiful could it be
It twinkles on the water bright
When I go back home in the night.

Jessie's poem 13 April 1994
Her last day at school

Author's
FOREWORD

My memories of Jessie remain lively even though I had only a few months to be acquainted with her. I clearly recall the phone call that invited me to offer 'healing prayer' for a nine-year old with an inoperable brain tumour. My first reaction was panic. I had never met her, even though she lived nearby. I knew her parents, Alan George and Lesley Schatzberger, only as professional musicians. What was I to do as a 'praying healer'? (This title still jars me when I see it in Jessie's address book!) How was I to pray in a home where the family was not Christian? My understanding was that in their desperation to seek help of a more alternative type, my name had been given to them as someone who could pray.

In February 1994, on a cold Monday morning in York, I ventured over to Yvonne Seymour's home. As a friend of mine, she agreed to introduce me to her neighbours. We walked from Yvonne's home at Number 11 next door to the Georges at Number 10. Upon knocking, my anxieties eased as a vivacious girl, puffy with steroids, answered and led me into the kitchen to introduce me to her mother, Lesley. She then showed me pictures that her class at school had painted for her. Next she let me pet her cats, glance at her books, and peek at a few photos. To my delight, I didn't need to say very much at all and I began to draw warmth from being with her. Jessie was not only a good talker, she was also a natural leader. After finishing the introductions, she told me about her tumour and how it was growing much too quickly and large.

Even with all this information, I still had no idea how to initiate praying on her behalf. Once again, Yvonne provided the solution to my dilemma. She offered to massage Jessie's feet later in the day. I jumped in with my offer to put my hands on her head then and there and to say a prayer for her. She liked both ideas.

Jessie climbed onto her mother's lap, and I cupped my hands round her head. Trying to relax and listen for an appropriate prayer, I finally found some words addressed to the Creator who made our heads and our brains. When I stated that an unwelcome intruder had invaded Jessie's head, she jumped right into the middle of the prayer to inform me that she had named her tumour 'Blob'. From that intervention onward, Jessie became the guide and I the one who responded to her leading. From her, I gained new insight into Jesus' wise words that 'a child shall lead us.'

For the next few months, I returned on a regular basis to pray with and for Jessie. Sadly, it became clear that Jessie was not going to be cured, not even by prayer. his was no indication that together we had not experienced any value in praying. On the contrary, after each prayerful encounter, Jessie was the first to express the peace and a sense of presence that met with us. I last saw Jessie the night before she died in Martin House Children's Hospice. On this occasion she offered me one of the fairy cakes that she asked the cook to bake. After eating the bun, I knew that I should pray, but I felt awkward because other members of Jessie's family were playing with a nearby computer. Always before,

I had prayed for her in the privacy of their home. I drove back to York feeling sad, not only because of my own lack of confidence, but because I sensed that it would be my last time with this intriguing little girl. This proved to be true, and I attended her funeral at Martin House on 9th May 1994.

My friendship with the Georges deepened along with my desire to be supportive of them as a family. During the months that Lesley and Alan had been caring for Jessie, generous friends and family members had supported them financially. When a treatment for Jessie in America had looked like a possibility, the funds increased. Within a few months after her death, these unused funds were diverted into a charity providing music therapy to work in children's hospices. Within a decade, eleven music therapists working in the hospices produced the book *Music Therapy in Children's Hospices: Jessie's Fund in Action.*

In the Autumn of 2003, Lesley told me about the publication. It occurred to me that many people benefiting from this work would have very little, if any, knowledge of the child who had given her name to the charity. When I questioned Lesley, she looked at me and declared that I should be the one to write stories about her daughter. In pursing the challenge, Jessie began to reveal herself to me even more deeply as I interviewed her friends and family.

Through these investigative encounters with people who knew and loved Jessie, I was reminded that the memories we hold and cherish do not always match the facts. I shall always remember my first interview with her school friend, Susie Hoyland, who vividly described how she and Jessie had accidentally dropped a book into the basement flat.

Jessie's Story

When I investigated the practicalities of this misadventure, I discovered that the interior of the house would not actually allow the book to disappear as she remembered. Susie's memory, however, held true for her as a vivid incident in her friendship with Jessie. On other occasions, I encountered conflicting information within family members' stories.

Eventually, I decided to write little 'snippets' or vignettes in Jessie's life. Instead of focusing on the 'facts', I would create the dialogue based on my grasp of Jessie's personality. I had met with no lack of agreement or disharmony with friends and family when it came to describing her personality traits. To all who knew and loved her, she was clearly a creative child with determination, forthrightness, perfectionist tendencies, and a definite need to be right—in a most loving and winsome manner. She loved life and tenaciously clung to making every day as full as possible. Sadly, Blob had other ideas.

I hope that these stories introduce readers to the child who gave her name to Jessie's Fund, and may reawaken memories in those who knew and loved her.

Sharon Stinson
All Souls Day 2005
York

Heartfelt
ACKNOWLEDGEMENTS

Thank you, Jessie.

This adventure of writing about you has been made possible by your inspiring personality which continues to live in and through your writings, photos, friends, and family. The more I ventured into the little incidents I have selected to write about, the more I discovered your free spirit, one that in many ways defied social convention. (For your own poems and journal entries, I remained true to your free spelling, puctuation, and grammar.)

Thank you, Jessie's family.

Lesley Schatzberger has been a faithful source of information and companionship. She has corrected my misconceptions and influenced my many revisions.

Alan George has searched through data for specific dates and places while frequently laughing his way through the stories.

Hannah George offered a major realignment when I was drifting off course—even though she wasn't aware of her valuable contribution.

Jacob George, the longed-for brother that Jessie never knew, grabbed each draft and read it quietly and lovingly and didn't hesitate to offer suggestions from his own unique perspective.

Jessie's Story

Rosl Schatzberger, Jessie's Oma, drew from the well-springs of her memory specific images and actions that enabled me to visualize Jessie much more clearly in many scenes and situations.

Joyce George, Jessie's other grandmother, sat with me at the table showing and describing objects given her by Jessie. She recalled the joy of Jessie's visits to her home in Cornwall.

These family members have allowed me a place amongst them as together we enjoyed the memory of Jessie reawakened through these stories. I am most grateful to each of them.

Thank you, Jessie's friends.

I thoroughly delighted in interviewing people who knew Jessie:

Susie Hoyland and Julia Callan, two of her school friends;

Kate and May Stancliffe, her neighbourhood friends;

Myra Adshead (Nana) and Yvonne Seymour, mother and daughter, who live next door to the Georges;

Lucy Russell and Jose Honing, friends and musicians.

All of these people have willingly furnished me with more stories than I have been able to include.

Thank you, my friends.

Consistently I have sought out people to read the drafts from a more objective perspective.

Christine Tuck has been literally stopped in her tracks many times as I

Acknowledgements

put the latest story in front of her.

Sandy Goodwill, Gordon Murray, Roger Lake, and Miles Salter, my writing group companions, offered supportive comments and encouraging presence—especially when I cooked them a tasty meal.

When the time came to have someone proof the text, I knew that I could call upon Alison Phelps. She welcomed the challenge while opening my eyes to greater clarity and insights.

My California Goddaughter, Karyn Wolf Lynn, became my editor, advisor and publisher. Her professional acumen continues to astonish and affirm me. With her help, I came to believe in the possibility of *Jessie's Story* being available to those who not only know Jessie's Fund, or have benefited from hospices, but to those of us who recall times in our lives when our spirits were freer and less cluttered by social conventions.

Sharon Stinson

Jessie's story

Shells, shells on the sea shore,
Shells, shells getting more and more
Different shapes and different sizes,
Some could even make good prizes.

From Jessie's poem, February 1994

Went to clinic in the morning at Cookridge hospital, (in Leeds)
and got given an easter egg by one of the kind nurses. After that
we went to a restaurant and I had PIZZA. When we got home, Mum took
me to Maggie's (my homeopath.) She said I was looking very well.
Then I watched Neighbours.

Journal entry dated March 31, 1994

chapter one
A TRUNK OF MEMORIES

'I'm not sure I can be doing with this,' Alan said as he and Lesley sat down in front of a trunk in one of the second floor bedrooms. It was 7th October 2003 and I was hoping that by looking at Jessie's things, Lesley and Alan might have memories awakened. I needed to learn more about the daughter I had known for only a few months before her death.

Unhurriedly, Lesley lifted the lid. Various items of clothing were carefully folded near the top of the large trunk. Exploring beneath them, she discovered a pair of slippers made of soft hide and lined with sheepskin. 'These would fit Jacob,' she commented, putting them to one side.

Alan agreed, 'I think he'd like to wear them. Actually they are quite like mine.'

Lesley lifted out the top shelf of the trunk where notebooks, autograph books, a colouring book and school records had been kept safe. 'You might like to read these, Sharon.' Then she brought out a silk blue-grey scarf. 'I gave Jessie my scarf. When she was ill, she loved the feel of the silk and the smell of it. It seemed to give her lots of comfort. It was like giving her something of me.' She handed me the scarf so that I could fondle it.

'I don't know if I can open this or not,' Lesley said, as she felt the contents of a carrier bag through the outside. Cautiously she brought out a plastic mask made especially for Jessie's face to keep her head absolutely still during treatments at the Cookridge Radiotherapy Unit in Leeds. I asked Alan how he felt about seeing it. 'It's a piece of plastic,' he responded, turning his head away.

Lesley continued to explore the contents of the trunk. 'Oh, here's the amethyst necklace that Yvonne Seymour gave Jessica.' Attached to the necklace was a small piece of paper telling in detail the healing powers of amethyst. After reading the description, Lesley added, 'It didn't work wonders,' as she put the gift back into its box.

Another bag had some knitting and two 8" knitting needles in it. 'All her life Jessica liked to make things. My mother taught her how to cook, knit, and sew. Just before she died, Jessica began to make jewellery to sell and raise money for her treatment, which of course never happened. So any money earned or donated became part of Jessie's Fund.'

'Our two girls were so different,' Lesley reminisced, "Chubby" Hannah danced with grace, and talked freely from the age of one. Jessie was slim, but definitely not graceful with her heavy feet and a noisy, stomping walk. You know, she didn't talk until she was two; then she immediately used full sentences.'

'And when she did start talking, she didn't respond with simply "yes" or "no",' added Alan. She would say, "Yes, I am going to do that."'

'Chalk and cheese, they were, and that is what made them enjoyable to watch when they did their little performances,' continued Lesley.

Then she went on to describe how the girls loved to arrange chairs in the music room, put dolls on each of the chairs, and then invite their parents in to watch them perform. They didn't bother to write scripts; they simply loved to dance and act spontaneously. Jessie smeared bright lipstick well past her lipline to exaggerate her mouth. 'Larger than life as usual,' remembered her father.

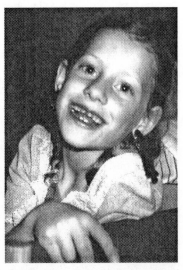

Jessie dressed up with bright lipstick and dangling earrings

Alan then recalled that wherever they travelled in Europe, for example, with the English Baroque Soloists, the girls searched out stages in the villages so that they could clamber up the wooden stairs and offer impromptu performances. 'I remember they did this in a village in Austria, Durnstein, which was having a summer festival. Our girls could attract quite an audience.'

'They did it in Italy and other places as well. We would be slightly embarrassed, but we couldn't help but be doting parents,' said Lesley.

'Sorry that we can't remember more. You'll need to ask her grandparents and friends.' With this comment, Lesley put each of the precious items back inside the trunk; all except the slippers for Jacob. As we walked down the stairs, Alan stopped in front of a painting of Jessie, 'See, she is wearing the blue-grey scarf.'

'Soft and made of silk, ' I added. ❧

Thursday 6th June

me:

I have got one sister called hannah. I have got one pet kitten called paddy. I have got blue eyes. my mummy has greeny eyes. my daddy has got brown eyes. my sister has got brown eyes too. my best friends are alice susie and diana and some others. I like miss Lamb very very much. my mummy is calld Lesley. my daddy is calld Alan. I am six years old. I LIKe the School I go to very very very Much. the best things I like to eat is spaghetti and afew other things. my sister is Sometimes alot of a nuisance. I like to play alot of different Kinds of Games. I have got fair hair. I like having fair hair.

Chapter Two
JESSIE WRITES ABOUT HER FAMILY

Thursday 6th June

me.

I have got one sister called hannah. I have got one pet kitten called paddy. I have got blue eyes. my mummy has greeny eyes. my daddy has got brown eyes. my sister has got brown eyes too. my best friends are alice suse and diana and some others. I like miss Lamb very very much. my mummy is calld Lesley. my daddy is calld Alan. I am six years old. I like the school I go to very very very Much. the best things I like to eat is spaghetti and afew other thingsmy sister is sometimes alot of a nuisance. I like to play alot of different kinds of Games. I have got fair hair. I like having fair hair. ∝

When I go to MacDonalds I eat Hamburger and chips,
I never forget to give them their tips.
I always drink lemonade
And I always find a place in the shade.

From Jessie's poem "MacDonald's"

Chapter Three
JESSIE AND DANIEL

Oma shook the doorknob. The door to the cloakroom refused to budge. Listening carefully, Jessie's Viennese grandmother heard water running from inside the little room. She wasn't sure if it was the toilet or the tiny washbasin, but she sensed danger. Inside, Jessie and her next door playmate were up to something. Being careful not to upset the children, she tried to entice them to stop playing. 'Jessie, I've baked you and Daniel some biscuits. Come out now.'

'We can't, Oma. The door won't open,' giggled Jessie.

'Slide the bolt, Gucki', ordered Oma. She used a pet name that in Viennese means 'looking, seeing' and was inspired by Jessie's vivid blue eyes. Nothing happened. Becoming aware of her slightly quickening heart beat, she muttered to herself not to get upset.

Oma walked quickly back to the kitchen where she kept a pad of paper and pencil on the oval table while she was sitting with her grandchildren. Grabbing these, she drew a picture of the door and the bolt. Making bold arrows, she indicated the direction to move the bolt. 'They'll be ok. Don't be afraid,' she repeated her mantra of calming words. Suddenly she remembered that Nana, Daniel's Yorkshire gran, would soon be coming along the back garden path connecting the two houses. She would be prompt in collecting Daniel for lunch.

If Nana knew that Daniel and Jessie were locked away and inaccessible, she would take action, probably using force to break down the door. Tiny and slight of build, Nana often stated unashamedly that she had worked physically hard all her life and that was the reason for being so strong. Oma differed in that she relied more on logic and reasoning to think through a tight corner situation. At this moment in time, she was letting her imagination run ahead of her thinking.

Rushing back to the cloakroom, she grumbled about Jessie's antics disrupting her baking day. What attracted her two-year-old granddaughter to seek out the oddest places to play? One adult could hardly find room to stand in the small cloakroom with the snugly fitting toilet and extra small basin taking most of the space. Her mind started magnifying the worst possible scenarios. What if Daniel and Jessie were climbing up on the new shelves that Lesley had built? Lesley kept the toilet cleaner and other solvents on the shelves. Inadvertently they may be spilling the chemicals and burning their young, tender skin. The vacuum cleaner, stored beneath the shelves, could also be damaged if any of the solvents broke open. Logic and reason escaped Oma as her panic took over. This would-be-playroom housed dangers that these 'little uns'—as Nana called them—might be facing unawares. She thought she could hear water running, possibly flooding the room.

Slipping her sketch under the door, she said, 'Jessie, I've drawn you a picture. Look at it and then try to slide the bolt on the door.'

Oma heard Daniel and Jessie laugh as they jiggled the lock. Nothing happened. The bolt refused to budge. Looking at the clock, she realized that in less than twenty minutes Nana would be collecting Daniel.

Happy friends

Reluctantly but desperately, Oma dialled 999. 'Two small children, a boy and girl, they're only just over two years old, are locked in a toilet, a cloakroom. Can you help please? I can't get them out.' While waiting for the rescuers, Oma walked back and forth between the kitchen and the cloakroom waiting anxiously for help. Then it occurred to her that if she started to sing nursery rhymes, she could encourage Jessie and Daniel to sing along with her. They could stay happily unaware of their imminent danger. Only recently she had taught them 'Ten Green Bottles' with all its verses. Singing loudly, she encouraged Jessie and Daniel to sing along.

The unmistakeable sound of the fire engines stopped Oma's singing. She looked out of the front door to see, not one, but two, engines completely blocking the narrow street. Two fire fighters advanced toward her as she waved at them from the front door of Number 10. Her quick and detailed assessment enabled the men to move into action instantly. 'We'll need to remove the narrow sash window so we can put a pole in to move the bolt,' said one of the firemen.

Just as the fire fighters were dragging their ladders up to the small window, Nana opened the front door next door at Number 11. Shaking her duster, she gasped at the sight of the fire engines. 'Jessie's 'ouse is on fire. My little Daniel and wee Jessie…Oh dear. Oh, dear. What's goin' on?' Yelling at the men, she flew down the steps to the pavement.

'It's all right, love. Just two little ones got locked in the toilet. Don't worry, we'll have them out in no time at all.'

'Nana, come in. Come, have a cup of tea. I didn't tell you because I didn't want to worry you,' called Oma.

Nana's Yorkshire expressions flew out so quickly that Oma could hardly grasp what she was saying. Seeing the fire fighters, she had immediately feared for the life of her Daniel in a house on fire. 'Oma, you and me, we're taking care of these little uns together. We're s'pose to make sure they are okay. What would our Yvonne say? Oh dear. Oh dear.'

'You know Jessie and Daniel love playing in the cloakroom, but they locked the door and couldn't slide the bolt back.'

'You shud've called me. Oma, I cud've shook that door open. I'd 've got 'em out.'

'I drew them a picture trying to show them how to slide the bolt....'

Just then Jessie and Daniel danced into the kitchen. Jessie, as usual, did all the talking and Daniel nodded his head in agreement. Following close behind them was a firefighter. Oma, greatly relieved, invited the rescuers to sit down and have tea and biscuits with all of them.

'We don't have time right now. You'll need to have the window replaced. We've got another call, so we must get going. You children okay?'

Jessie looked at the big tall man and spoke with her usual confidence. 'We play in the loo.'

'Well don't lock the door anymore when you go in there. We got you out this time, but next time you might have to stay in there much longer.'

'Daniel and Jessica, come here and sit down,' said Oma. 'I've got some lovely egg and toasty soldiers for your lunch, and then you can have a piece of Guglhupf cake.'

'Daniel, don't ya ever do that again. That's upset Nana.' She reached down and pulled her grandson onto her knee to give him a cuddle.

Nana reverted to her well-established pattern. She insisted that after they finished their lunch, her two little un's, having played together, must be put into the deep, double sinks in the basement kitchen to soak in hot water. 'Warm water is 'ealthy,' said Nana, certain of her cure. Then once again, she returned her grandson to spend the remainder of the day with his friend and Oma.

Two hours later, baths taken, and calmness prevailing, the doorbell of Number 10, rang long and hard. Oma grabbed Jessie to stop her from running ahead to answer it. 'We're from the *York Evening Press*. We understand that two little children got locked in the loo. Could you tell us about it?'

Inviting the reporter and the photographer to come in, Oma started to tell them what had happened, but Jessie jumped in ahead of her.

'We play in the loo. He's my friend,' pointing at Daniel.

'Could you show us where you were playing?' asked the reporter.

'In here,' said Jessie, pulling Daniel behind her.

'You show me and we'll take a picture of you both,' said the photographer standing in the hall and leaning inside the door as the two-year-olds squeezed into the tiny space.

Late that evening, after Jessie was asleep upstairs in Number 10, and Daniel tucked in his bed at Number 11, Lesley and Alan returned home. Oma, exhausted and burdened from the events of the day, showed them the evening newspaper.

'Mum, all you had to do was insert a knife in between the door and

Jessie and Daniel   Photo courtesy of York and County Press

the doorpost to slide the bolt away from the catch. I'll show you,' said Lesley as she demonstrated the easy way out to her mother.

'I could have saved myself and Nana all that anxiety and panic and you would not have to pay for a window replacement. You must tell me these things ahead of time, Lesley.'

Looking at the *Evening Press,* Alan said proudly, 'That's a great little photo. We'll save that one.' ଔ

My Small Poem

My poem is neat,
But very petite,
So that's why I call it sweet,
You know it's got nothing
to do with feet.

Chapter Four
ABBEY ROAD STUDIOS

Jessie with Oma outside the flat in Leyton

As soon as Oma pulled the door to the flat shut, she knew what she had done. She had locked the key and her handbag inside. No one else had a key except her daughter—miles away—and not to be disturbed under any condition. How could she possibly keep two little girls entertained for a whole day in the depressing heat of London? All she had planned to do was walk to the nearby greengrocer. Thankfully, she had her purse with her.

Three-year-old Jessie started asking questions just when her grandmother needed time to get her head around a plan. 'Where are we going? It's too hot outside. Let's go back in. Will you read to me from my fairy story book?' Hannah, two years older than Jessie, started to drift down the street, unaware of her grandmother's dilemma.

Oma shook the door several times. It wouldn't budge. Only last month the George family had purchased this flat in Leyton after selling the leaky old Bedford Motor Caravan—their home for the previous six months while their lives as musicians kept them on the road. Adjusting to a new place proved more complicated than Oma had calculated. What would she do now? She dreaded the thought of disturbing Lesley now at the Abbey Road Studios recording 'The Fantastic Symphony'.

Seeing no way out of her disaster, Oma and the girls would have to get a key from Lesley. But how? She didn't know how to find the studio. How would she move about a big city with Jessie's pushchair and Hannah's reluctance to walk for long distances? London's morning heat oppressed both her and the complaining girls.

'Oma it's hot. Let's go back to York,' whined Jessie.

Just before Lesley had left early to catch the underground, she reminded her mother of the restrictions put on her day. 'Remember that I can't be interrupted during this recording. At Abbey Road the recording costs are based on units of time and each one costs a fortune. Of course, let me know if something really worrying happens. Leave word with the receptionist and I'll check with him when we have a break.' These were Lesley's last words. Now what was Oma to do? She needed time to think. She shook the locked door again.

'Get *Winnie the Pooh* for me', Hannah called out as she hopped back to Jessie and her grandmother.

A book! The library! That's it! Oma had noticed a library just a few streets away. The reference section would have all the information she needed. Once she found out the address of the studios, someone could help her to decide on the best way to get to the other side of London. All would be well when Lesley gave her a key, and then the three of them could find a park to cool off with a picnic. Of course, after the reference section, she would have to stop in the children's section to read a story to the girls. And she did exactly that.

Leaving the library, Oma struggled to manage two small girls and a pushchair on the busy streets and crowded London public transport. Jessie grumbled as they moved toward the Underground Station. 'No tube, Oma. Too crowded. Too many people. I don't like the tube.'

Resisting Jessie's objections, Oma assured her that the tube wouldn't be too full during this time of day, and besides it was a much faster way to get across a big city. She put some water onto her handkerchief to cool Jessie's face as she directed the girls on to the train.

Leaving the second underground station, Oma manoeuvred the awkward pushchair down the street singing, 'Jack and Jill went up the hill….' But when Oma saw the road sign, she stopped needing to entertain the girls. What a relief.

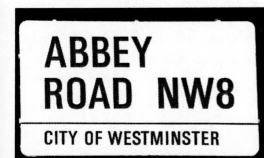

Arriving at the Abbey Road Studios, Oma approached the receptionist. 'My daughter, Lesley

Schatzberger, is recording here today with John Eliot Gardiner. When they have a break, will you let her know that her mother is here? Please do not interrupt her now. I'll be waiting with her two daughters in the café.'

'Hannah's being sick, Oma,' said Jessie pulling her grandmother's skirt.

Just at the moment, a colleague of the Georges came to their rescue. Chi-Chi put her arms around Hannah to lift her up to the basin. .

'You feel better now, Hannah?' asked Jessie, after Chi-chi set Hannah back down.

Finding a seat in the café, Oma ordered a cup of black coffee. Just then a voice boomed over the tannoy: 'Lesley Schatzberger, please come to reception.'

'That's my mummy. I want to see her,' said Jessie.

Within minutes, Lesley ran into the café to find her mother and daughters sitting at a table. 'Mummy, Mummy,' Jessie yelled loudly. She held out her hands to her mother.

Oma explained her need for a key. Lesley gave her mother the key out of her pocket and said, 'I must return to the recording now.'

'No Mummy. Don't go. I want to be with you. Let me come,' insisted Jessie who began to cry more and more loudly.

'Jessie and Hannah, you stay with Oma,. I must go now. I'll see you at the flat as soon as I can.' She turned away and walked briskly back toward the studio door.

'Jessie, be quiet. Your screams will interfere with the recording. Quiet.' Oma put Jessie in her pushchair and moved to the reception desk. 'Please order a taxi for me.'

In the taxi, the driver started to chat with the girls. 'Did you see the pictures of the Beatles? I used to come here in the 60's to see the boys when they recorded at the Abbey Road Studios. You girls like the Beatles?'

'My mummy was recording there. She plays the clarinet.

As the taxi approached Leyton, Oma remembered why she'd left home earlier and asked the driver to stop at the greengrocer near the flat.

'Oma, check your pocket. Do you have mummy's key? We can't get in the flat without the key. We've got to get in this time. Let me see it, Oma,' demanded Jessie. 'You locked us out, didn't you?' ❀

Listen to the Fathers great big frown
When you are watching great Blow Your House Down.
Listen to the big loud Rocket
Whilst you're eating sweets from your pocket.

From Jessie's poem 'November 5th'

Chapter Five
AT THE KONZERTHAUS

Taking hold of her granddaughter's hand to stop her from pushing her tiny weight against the heavy double doors of the concert hall, Oma said, 'We must be very quiet inside. Don't make any noise at all or we will have to leave. Your mother is rehearsing with a very important man. You must sit still and no talking. Do you understand, Jessie? Hannah?'

Jessie looked up at Oma, 'It's all right Oma. We've been to many rehearsals before. We know lots of conductors and musicians. We'll be quiet. We already know that Mummy is playing with Stockhausen. He is a composer and a conductor.'

'You're right, of course, Jessie,' said Oma aware that once again she had been gently corrected by this five year old. The heavy double doors forced Oma to push with all her strength to open them as she herself tried not to make any disturbing noises. Inside, the darkness was blinding. Only an isolated area on the distant stage radiated a soft light. Thousands of empty seats, row after row, waited in mysterious emptiness. Without people, without light, the place felt scary and creepy. Finally, Jessie's eyes adjusted to the dark and she looked toward the front to spot the conductor behind the electronic amplification desk.

On stage, Lesley strained to look into the blackness longing to see if

Lesley and Karlheinz Stockhausen

her daughters had arrived. A moment later, she forced herself to concentrate on *Michaels Reise* ,the demanding piece on her music stand. She couldn't afford to be distracted, even though somewhere among the thousands of deep velvet seats her Jessie and Hannah might be looking up at her. How thankful she felt that her mother had graciously agreed to bring them with her to Vienna. Lesley couldn't stop herself from listening for sounds in the vast theatre. She would recognize Jessie by her sure giveaway; her husky, throaty cough. As the notes on the music raced by, Lesley managed a deep breath and a quick moistening of her clarinet reed. Trying to stop thinking of her daughters was proving difficult. She began to calculate how she could arrange for Jessie and Hannah to talk for a few minutes with Karlheinz Stockhausen, a musician whose energy and dynamism enraptured many Europeans. What a privilege it was to play with him in the Konzerthaus in Vienna.

In the back row on the left side of the hall, Oma became aware of her youngest granddaughter standing up and sitting down repeatedly. Jessie fiddled on the seat in front of her with the rack to hold opera glasses, and then she lifted her own seat to see what secrets might be kept under it. When her boredom got the best of her, she whispered directly into her grandmother's ear, 'I want a drink, Oma.' Letting out a sigh of irritation, Oma stood up, gently pushed Jessie in front of her, took hold of Hannah's hand behind her, and silently stumbled with them through the darkness, back out through the heavy double doors, and finally into the light of the foyer.

'Now, what's the problem, Jessie? You want a drink of water? I thought that you wanted to see your mummy. What makes you so fidgety?' Looking around for some place of refuge, she noticed the empty bar. 'Let's go and sit there. I'll get you a drink and you and Hannah can read your books.' Both girls began to twirl about. 'We've been sitting a long time, Oma, we need to *do* something.' Within minutes, they took over the table and chairs in the bar to play one of their favourite games, 'Waitresses.'

'Oma, do you have a handkerchief? I need to put it over my arm.'

'You're a lucky girl, I have a clean one, Gucki,' said Oma.

'Do you have another one, for Hannah?' demanded Jessica.

'Do you think I am always equipped for every little game you play?' said Oma with a smile, as she handed over another clean handkerchief.

'Thank you, Oma, I knew you would have more than one,' said Jessie with a little bow. 'Now may I take your order, please? Are you ready? Have you looked at the menu?'

Relieved that the girls were finally being entertained, Oma opened the morning newspaper. Just then she caught a glimpse of a friend she had telephoned earlier. How good it would be to catch up with Elsa, hear the latest gossip—in German, of course—and find out about their Viennese relatives. The girls moved about the empty bar with their *menu of the day* carrying their white towels over their arms as they served imaginary customers. Just as the two women were getting comfortable, it seemed that all of the girls' customers had been served.

Jessie cut into the adult conversation with, 'Oma, I'm hungry.'

Once again Oma had to make a change in her plans and accommodate her granddaughters. Bundling the girls into their coats, hats, and scarves, the four of them left the Konzerthaus. Instantly the icy breeze and blowing snow presented a struggle for the next quarter of an hour.

'I see a doughnut shop,' Jessie cried out. 'Let's get one, please, Oma.'

Once satisfied with the sugar-covered treats, they hurried back to the warmth of the hall. Elsa expressed a keen interest in catching the last part of the rehearsal. Oma put her fingers to her lips and said, 'Quiet', as she pushed once again through the double doors. In the darkness of the auditorium, she selected four seats in one of the back rows. Within a few seconds, the two adults became engrossed in listening to the intriguing music. When a pause came, Oma glanced around to see how her girls were managing. In the dark, she could make out only her older granddaughter.

'Hannah, where is Gucki?' Oma asked.

'She was here, but I don't know where she went.'

'Elsa, keep an eye on Hannah, please.' Oma stood in the aisle looking for the proverbial needle in the haystack. Which one of the thousands of empty theatre chairs would be hiding her tiny Jessica? How could she possibly spot a small child among the alphabetical rows, the columns of aisles and the thousands of seats? At the same time, she was keenly aware that no one should be walking around in this hall during rehearsal. Jessie should have asked permission to leave her seat. Oma strained her wide-open eyes. Her heart raced wildly. She lifted each foot to walk soundlessly down the aisle. If only she could call out. If only she had a torch and could direct it between the seats.

Oma's mind began to imagine all sorts of possibilities. Maybe Jessie had left the hall and gone out into the street again. She knew the way to the doughnut shop. Talking rationally to calm down, she admitted that in no way could Jessie manage those heavy doors on her own. She had to be somewhere in the hall. As Oma got nearer to the illuminated area, her fear increased. She felt like a spy, an intruder. Could she advance her search to another aisle without being spotted by Stockhausen? Bending down to see the letter of the row, she bumped her knee against the seat and pulled back in pain. She could hear Stockhausen's fingers turning the buttons on the desk as he adjusted the amplification. With her fear now on red-alert, Oma raised up to her full height to catch a glimpse of his hands moving rapidly over the control board. For a moment, she was transfixed by the wonder of his artistic ability. Fear jerked her back into reality. What if he sensed her presence? She felt like a naughty school girl. Lesley might be able to see her moving about. In spite of her heart beating in her ears, she couldn't resist looking at the blond hair and dramatic facial features of the famous composer.

Stockhausen stopped moving the controls. He had heard her! She
turned to rush quietly back up the side aisle just as she saw him lift both
hands toward the musicians on the stage. Then he lowered them and
put one hand in his right pocket. Out came a handkerchief. He wiped
his forehead. Oma held her breath, pulled down a seat in Row B and
started to sit down so that she wouldn't be so obvious. It was then that
she noticed some movement near Stockhausen—just behind him in the
centre aisle. Focussing her gaze, Oma realized that it was a little girl--
close enough to reach out and touch the man. 'That's Gucki! What is
she doing there? I've got to get to her?'

With one athletic leap, Stockhausen bounded onto the stage. 'It's half-
one so we must stop. Have a pleasant lunch. Make sure that you get
some time to rest before being here for the performance at 8 p.m. You
have worked hard.'

Oma sidestepped through Row B and took Jessie firmly by the hand.
Walking up the centre aisle to join the others, she resisted scolding her
granddaughter in a public place. She would deal with her later.

Jessie looked up at her and grinned, 'I watched mummy playing. I could
see everything. Now I remember that I met Stockhausen before. I think
in Germany.' ∝

At the Konzerthaus

I want to be a musician playing on my world round trip
I want to be a rabbit, hippity hop hip hip.

From Jessie's poem 'I want to be...' February 1994

Chapter Six
THE VIOLINIST

Jessie refused to talk to anyone. Behind the piano in the music room, no one could see her in her distress, although anyone nearby might hear her sobs. She frequently sulked in a corner in the kitchen where everyone could see her. Today, however, was different. She couldn't display her feelings to any and everyone passing through the kitchen. The upright piano provided a dark place to veil her shame and embarrassment. In the darkness, she gave way to her heartbreak. She had failed.

Hannah, her confident sister, had not failed. Even while Jessie suffered, Hannah was searching diligently to find a decorative picture frame in which to hang her certificate. Once on display for others to admire, she eagerly waited for their compliments. Life wasn't fair. Hannah, in spite of not practising nearly as much as her younger sister, got the higher accolade: a Distinction in Grade 3 Flute.

From the beginning when Jessie, aged five, began to take lessons, Jose Honing, her violin teacher, recognised her as a natural musician. Jose said more than once to Alan and Lesley, 'Your little girl can make a jolly good sound.' Her pupil picked up tunes quickly and delighted in playing them. Practising scales, however, was another thing. Lesley over and over stressed the value in learning the different key scales. Jessie heard but promptly ignored her mother's wisdom. On the other hand, when it came to performing of any kind, Jessie had no problem at all. Ever since she could walk, Jessie sought out centre stage places—either ready-built stages or make-believe ones. She loved to dance, to act, or simply to call the world to attention. After all, she lived with professional musicians and grew up knowing that all the world was a stage. If she were to try and count the number of professionals that came through their front door, she would quickly lose track. Then of course, she had also attended innumerable concerts where she observed performers. Being on stage was normal. Good performances brought praise. Today praise was not allowed.

'Keep away from me, everyone, Hannah, Mummy, Daddy. I especially don't want to see Lucy when she comes.' Lucy Russell, her older friend and violinist, had always consoled and encouraged her. She too was forbidden access to the back of the piano. Certainly, Jessie didn't want Jose to see her. Jose must be fed up with her. She had utterly let down her teacher who taught her so well.

'Stand correctly, Jessie,' Jose had said, making sure that she instructed her pupil in all aspects of musicianship. She couldn't help but notice her petite pupil's polished shoes and neatly pressed dress. At this request, Jessie promptly straightened her spine and increased her height.

'Is this the proper way, Jose? This is how I have seen my daddy hold his viola.' Jessie knew how to elicit praise from her beloved teacher.

'Yes, Jessie, now you look ready to play.' For over thirty years, Jose had carefully observed St Peter's School pupils beginning to learn the violin. This pupil, however, was particular, perhaps a bit too fastidious, Jose thought. Jessie began each lesson by ceremoniously removing the green silk scarf in which she had lovingly wrapped her violin. Then, as

New Year's Eve 1992   Photo by Paul Schatzberger

if picking up a newborn baby out of its pram, she stooped to lift her
eighth size instrument out of the case. 'You are right and proper, Jessie,
but you really do not need to be quite so fussy,' complained Jose, trying
to break through the weekly ritual.

Jessie's story

With the first couple of years of lessons complete, Jessie had looked forward to taking the Grade 2 Violin Examination. On the day of the examination, Jessie walked hand in hand with her mother to the York Friend's Meeting House on Clifford Street. Jessie walked with uneasy steps, out of rhythm with her natural self. Sensing the nervous tension in her seven-year-old, Lesley, who trusted the effectiveness of herbal medicines, put a few drops of *Rescue Remedy* on Jessie's tongue to calm her while they waited her turn. As soon as Jessie heard the examiner call her name, she stretched on tip toes to give Lesley a quick hug and kiss. Jose stood waiting to walk into the room with her as her accompanist. Her mother, meanwhile, would wait on tenterhooks in the foyer with fingers crossed.

Something strange and uneasy stirred within her as she approached the room to be tested. She didn't recognize the ancient and unfamiliar intruder who made a direct attack. From out of the blue, shot a dart of stage fright, injecting her with timidity and crushing her confidence. When she lifted her fiddle, her slight body switched into someone rigid and wooden. Her fingers stiffened on the bow. On the page of music in front of her, the notes stayed readable, but her tense body kept her from playing in her naturally relaxed manner. Even *Rescue Remedy* couldn't calm her.

Jose put a reassuring arm around her as they walked heavily away from the examiner. Once again, Jose felt confirmed in her philosophy that forbid her Grade 1 pupils from taking the exam. Now, being present with Jessie, she questioned the rightness of Grade 2. 'It's wait-and-see time, Jessie,' said Jose, feeling slightly guilty that she had subjected her to the ordeal.

The next day, and for the two next weeks, eager to learn the results, Jessie raced to collect the letters dropped through the flap in the door. Finally, after an eternity, she recognized the envelope. Getting the letter knife to open it, she instantly sank into despair as the words in capital letters leapt out at her: MERIT FOR GRADE 2 VIOLIN. Having dismissed from her mind the tension of the exam, she had fantasized about receiving a Distinction just like her sister Hannah. Somebody had made a mistake. How could the examiner have done this to her? Lowering her head and turning her back, she quietly withdrew from family and friends. No words of congratulations could erase the damned word, MERIT. Any expressions of comfort would ring false. She squeezed into the tiny space behind the piano where she could slide into shame to nurse her feelings of failure.

When Jose stopped by the George's, she spoke to her pupil from the keyboard side of the piano. She dare not invade the dark cave to look Jessie in the face. 'Jessie, I know that you are disappointed. You wanted a Distinction, and a Merit is not good enough for you. I want to tell you that your nerves kept you from getting a Distinction, not your talent. You are a good little violin player, but for the first time you now know what can happen when you get tense and anxious. We will work hard for Grade 3. You can learn to be more relaxed in testing situations.'

In time Jessie's cave became too restrictive as her heartbreak lessened. Crawling out from the darkness, she returned to the light with her outgoing self. Her sense of failure had diminished. By the time for her next lesson with Jose, she had reclaimed her confidence and regained her stance of being in charge. With her fiddle out of the case and the green scarf folded, she pressed onward and upward. 'Jose, let's play, "Twinkle, twinkle little star."'

Jose, attempting to emphasize her position as teacher, replied, 'I want to teach you a new folk song. I also have some carols for you to learn before Christmas, but you are going to have to practise your scales.'

'You know that I will practise scales. Right now, I'm in the mood to play tunes. Oh, Jose, I almost forgot. I brought you a present for accompanying me. I chose it myself.'

Jose, fully aware that Jessie ultimately decided the order of play, opened the carefully wrapped gift. 'How beautiful. A little cream jug. It's lovely. Thank you Jessie, I shall put it with the other gifts you have given me.' She stooped down to give her star pupil a warm hug.

'Ok, Jose. Now let's play, Twinkle, twinkle, little star. I've been practising it and I know that I do it really well. You'll be proud of me.'

'Very good, Jessie. Begin when you're ready.' ☙

The Violinist

Once upon a time there lived a little girl.
Her name was Lucy. One day she awoke and she had
a funny feeling...
she was very very very very happy.

From Jessie's Journal

chapter seven
JESSIE'S FRIEND LUCY

Three times in her short life, Jessie had the joy of being a bridesmaid. She adored these occasions because she loved being in the limelight with a fuss made over her. Jessie spun around in circles grinning with delight when Lucy asked her to be a bridesmaid in her wedding with Jonathan Tilbrook. This would be another chance to dress up and walk onto centre stage with so many guests looking favourably at her, and she would be sharing it with her special friend.

The year leading up to the wedding, Jessie and Lucy looked through bridal magazines that helped them to decide on what they found attractive and what they found ugly. Jessie hounded her mother and father to tell her all about their wedding. She even pestered her friends to learn about their parents' wedding days. One of the best parts was strolling through department stores with Lucy touching silk, satins and velvets while chatting endlessly through the details. Jessie insisted that the shoes must match the dress perfectly. As a bridesmaid-to-be, she totally involved herself in helping Lucy make her plans, and her friend didn't object most of the time. She enjoyed Jessie's keen interest.

Jessie was born shortly after Lucy arrived as a first term music student at the university. When Lucy was first introduced to baby Jessie, she knew that she would love her. Leaning over her , she said to her, 'You are gorgeous, and I am going to get to know you.' Her growing friendship

Lucy with Jessie age 4, before lessons

and frequent visits to the Georges provided many opportunities for her relationship with Jessie to flourish. Aged five, Jessie decided that she wanted to take violin lessons. After only a few lessons, she invited Lucy to play duets with her. Noticing how Jessie quickly learned to treat her little violin with infinitesimal care, Lucy readily agreed to allow Jessie to hold her own valuable full-size violin.

'Watch me, Lucy, I will hold it properly.' And of course she did.

Jessie treated her fair wavy hair as properly as she did her violin. At times, hair became an all-consuming focus of her day. 'Not a hair should be out of place' she insisted in her perfectionist approach to personal care.

'Lucy will you brush my hair? I want it to look nice. Do it like I've taught my mummy,' insisted Jessie.

'Jessie, are you aware how bossy you are? If I brush your hair, will you promise not to tease Hannah? The way you toss your hair in her face is not nice,' scolded Lucy. 'She is your sister and her hair is simply different from yours.'

'Well, you called her curls corkscrews. Is that nice?' Jessie made sure she had the last word. 'If you brush my hair now, I'll brush your hair later today.'

'The last time you brushed my hair, I nearly went bald,' Lucy said remembering how tender her head felt after Jessie's concentrated effort to have every hair perfect. 'I'd like some hair on my head for my wedding.'.

One day Alan and Lesley announced to their daughters that they would be going to Russia where Lesley would play with Karlheinz Stockhausen. Jessie jumped in and begged them to have Lucy and Jonathan come stay with Hannah and her. Knowing how hard their girls could be on *au pairs*, they agreed. What Lucy didn't know was that each morning, Jessie's built in alarm clock would wake her at 6.30 a.m. Daily she would spring out of bed, wake herself and everyone else by walking heavy footed around the house, and speaking loudly to herself in her deep, husky voice. If Lucy and Jonathan didn't stir within a few minutes, she would invade their room and snuggle up close to Lucy. Reluctantly awake, Lucy would look at her little friend's pale blue eyes and lovely shaped body and think to herself, 'You are going to be a beautiful woman—in spite of your Bugs Bunny front teeth'.

'Let's listen to Grieg's *Wedding March* today,' begged Jessie. 'I know we heard it yesterday, but I must hear it again. It will put us in a happy mood for your wedding.'

Lucy and her bridesmaids, Jessie and Hannah

'We also have to shop for your bridesmaid's shoes,' added Lucy.

'They must be white satin ones. Did you know that my mummy is sewing little white roses all around the neck and the sleeves of my satin turquoise dress, Lucy?' informed Jessie.

Going shopping with Jessie proved to be an adventure in itself. Jessie and her sister delighted the shopkeepers with their continual banter about the wedding. 'I feel like I am the bride,' said Jessie as she strutted around the shop trying on white satin shoes.

A few weeks before the wedding, Jessie went to London to stay in Lucy's home. Lucy wanted to make this a special occasion, so she carefully thought of all the things Jessie enjoyed. She set out a little table with paper and paints for her. When Jessie arrived, she immediately noticed how her friend had planned for her visit.

'Lucy, we are going to have a good time together. Look at these paints. I can paint something for you to hang on your wall.' When it came time to cooking a meal, Lucy invited Jessie to help her. 'I feel like it is a real treat entertaining you in my own home for a change,' Lucy told her little six-year-old friend.

Finally the big day arrived. On the wedding day of Lucy Russell and Jonathan Tilbrook, Jessie and Hannah revelled in the importance of being part of the inner sanctum. Walking down the aisle of the chapel at St Andrews University, Jessie looked around and with a queenly smile stole the hearts of those who had come to celebrate the occasion.

'How did I look, Lucy? Did I do my part well?' asked Jessie.

'Jessie, I want you to remember that this was my wedding day. How did I look? Actually, you looked adorable. I hope that I will be invited to your wedding.' ଔ

31ˢᵗ May   <u>Real</u>

Paris for the first
<u>time</u>

Summer 1990
I was five years old. I was really excited.
We were going to Paris, in France for the
first time. We were going to see my Mum, who
was at the time, playing her clarinet with John
Elliot Gardiners Orchestra. ~~at didnt~~ We
were going on the boat the next day.
My Dad was packing, Hannah was packing and
I was packing too. Hannah and I were
packing our bags with things to do, while
Dad, packing both ours and his suit cases.
It was the next day. We drove to Dover sea-port.
We got the HOVER-CRAFT. It took us about
forty minutes to get to the french sea-port. Now
Hannah and I, so excited we were
laughing our heads off. With a map of
course we drove to the square where
our hotel stood. It was called the Onion
We met my Mum and Lucy waiting for
us at the square. Oh By the Way
we always stay at the Onion. They
showed us, to it and our Dapartment.
We had a nice big Dapartment Wich was
quite pleasing because We had just about
inuff space to do what we wanted to get
done. The next morning We all found out
that we wanted to excersize our bodys.
We explored for quite a-bit and after
a while we found some quite intersting

- 44 -

Chapter Eight
JESSIE WRITES ABOUT PARIS

31 May   Real

Paris for the first time

Summer 1990

I was five years old. I was really excited. We were going to Paris
in France for the first time. We were going to see my Mum, who
was at the time, playing her clarinet with John Eeliot Gardiners
orcrestra. We were going on the boat the next day. My Dad was
packing, Hannah was packing and I was packing too. Hannah
and I were packing our bags with things to do, while Dad, packing
both ours and his suit cases. It was the next day. We drove to
Dover sea-port. We got the HOVER-CRAFT! It took us about forty
minutes to get to the french sea-port Noh Hannah and I, so
excited we were lauphing our heads off. With a map of-course
we drove to the square where our hotel stood. It was called the
Orion. We met my Mum and Lucy waiting for us at the square.

Jessie's Story

Oh By the way we always stay at the Orion. They showed us to
it and our Dapartment. We had a nice big Dapartment wich was
quite pleasing because we had just about inuff space to do what
we wanted to get done. The next morning we all found out that
we wanted to excersize our bodys. We explored for quite a-bit and,
after a while we found some quite interesting things. We found:
A strange, giant face sticking out of the ground with a big hand
next to it. We climbed on it. After that we finished our morning
strole by walking to the river. They when we got home we decided
to go to the shop and get some real French quasonts and yoghurt.
The week past quickly and before we new it, it was time to go,
home. I really enjoyed by first time in Paris. ∽

Jessie Writes About Paris

We had just about nuff space to do what we wanted to get done...
We found a strange, giant face sticking out of the ground...
The week passed quickly...
I really enjoyed my first time in Paris.

From Jessie's writing for school, 31 May 1990

Chapter Nine
HOLIDAY IN PARIS

On the long journey to Paris in the car laden with clothes, books, and games, Jessie had leaned forward to ask a question of her father and their conductor friend, Jonathan Tilbrook, 'What's the opera Mummy and Lucy are playing in this summer?'

Alan glanced over his shoulder at his younger daughter and replied, '*Cosi fan tutte, ossia la scuola degli amante.* It's an opera in two acts, a comedy. Try pronouncing that back to me.'

'*Cosi fan....* Well, what does it mean? Are we going to see it?'

'I'm not sure John Eliot or the concert hall will let you in, Jessie. It's called, *The School for Lovers*, and sometimes the title is, *They're all like that*,' smiled Alan as he grinned at Jonathan. 'It's for adults.'

'Well, it doesn't matter. I just wanted to be with Mummy and Lucy. I love to listen to them play. We'll see them at the Orion anyway. You will take me to my favourite merry-go-round, Daddy. This year I'm going to ride the white and pink horse.'

Arriving in Paris after the long journey, Jessie quickly unpacked her suitcase and then hopped noisily down the long hallway. First she jumped only on the red carpet tiles. Reaching the end of the long narrow passage, she did a pirouette, leaping this time onto the alternate grey tiles as she sang with uninhibited delight. For this her second visit, she planned to take in every enjoyment she could because she was back in the city of summer delights. In her husky voice, she sang louder with each hop, 'We're in Paris again! We're with Mummy, again! We're in the Orion again!'

Jessie sang joyfully within the Orion Apartment Hotel where members of the John Eliot Gardiner's orchestra stayed during their summers of playing Mozart's Operas in Paris. With children and parents staying together, the hotel became one big family—a place to relax, eat, and play together when not performing.

The next day, after settling into the Orion and being reunited with Lesley and the other musicians and children, Alan began to occupy his daughters with the wonders of Paris. Riding on the merry-go-round, Jessie screamed in her husky voice, 'Look Daddy, I'm riding without hands!' as her fair hair caught the breeze and blew around her head covering her eyes. Stepping off the ride, Alan noticed that Jessie was slightly dizzy from going round and round. Once he helped to steady her, she informed him that she was ready to go to the Pompidou Centre to see the Lips Fountain. Seeing the lips spout out water, Jessie began giggling. The humorous design enraptured her. She looked around at her family and pronounced, 'I name this our laughing place.' Having said that she started giggling again and all the others joined her.

Jessie loved surprises, and during this summer she had a very special one from one of the musicians. Liz Wilcock approached Lesley and Alan with an invitation from out of the blue. 'Would your girls like to join me and my three at the Disney Resort Hotel and have a couple of days in Euro Disney? You probably know that it just opened this year, and we have a spare hotel room-- that is, if they don't mind sharing with our *au pair*.'

When they opened the door at the Disney Hotel room, Jessie and Hannah walked into a dream, a fantasyland. 'Look Hannah, Tinker Bell,' squealed Jessie, pointing to the designs painted on the wardrobe. All over the walls and even on the bedspreads, Disney characters welcomed them into an atmosphere of play. 'It's magic. How will I ever be able to sleep?'

Not even two days of downpour could spoil their fairyland delight. Putting on rain gear, the five girls ran from one ride to another with Liz close behind. Floating in little boats through the canal, Jessie started the others off by singing along with 'It's a Small World'.

'Sleeping Beauty' inspired ooh's and ah's from the girls in spite of soggy, clinging, clothes. Moving from that event to the next, Liz's sandals became so wet and slippery that she couldn't walk properly. Suddenly she fell, breaking a strap on one of her sandals.

'Stop everyone. We must help Liz fix her broken sandals,' said Jessie, always ready to take charge. Liz managed to tie a knot in the leather strap before standing. She assured them that she wasn't hurt as she moved more cautiously. 'We must be at the gate to meet Lesley in a few minutes. I'm pleased that she'll have a chance to see this wonderful place with us.'

'We must take Mummy on the Alice in Wonderland Cups,' said Jessie. 'She'll love it, I'm sure.'

Left to right: Liz Wilcock, Francesca, Josie, Jessie, Lesley, Hannah, Bryony, at EuroDisney

When greeted with this itinerary at the gate, Lesley asked, 'Is it gentle?' 'I'm not used to going on fast rides.'

'I'm sure of it, Mummy. It's called Alice's Teacups or something like that. Let's go. You'll love it.'

As the seven of them crowded into one pink and purple cup with waves and hearts painted on the outside, the irregular spinning began. Forward and backward, round and round in random motion, they glided along unseen tracks. With an unpredictable surge to the right, they all leaned into each other only to be thrust in an unexpected u-turn to the left, plunging them into another surprise shift.

'Will this never end? It's more like a storm in a teacup,' Lesley pointed out.

'You can't fall out, Mummy. We are squeezing you safely,' assured her younger daughter.

'That was enough for me. I've never been so tossed about in my life,' moaned Lesley.

'We're okay now Mummy. Come on. Say it was fun!' teased Jessie as she reached for her mother's hand.

'We haven't been on the Pirates of the Caribbean,' said Liz, as she directed the recovering girls toward their final experience. 'We need to leave EuroDisney after this one.'

In the middle of the Caribbean ride, the thrill ended. Everything came to a grinding and complete halt. As they waited for motion to resume, the girls became restless. Complaints echoed from car to car. 'Our last hour and this happens,' muttered Liz.

Seeing an attendant checking the equipment, Jessie called out to him. 'This is our last ride. We have other things to see before we leave. Can't you make it run, please?'.

'*Pardon, ma petite. Je ne parle pas anglais.*'

Of course, the ride was ultimately fixed, and all too soon, they were leaving the EuroDisney make-believe world. Giving hugs and kisses to Bryony, Josephine and Francesca, Jessie and Hannah expressed their thanks to Liz for the marvellous two days in a world of fantasy.

'Franjessica, you tell your dad that he should come here and go on Space Mountain because we didn't have time for that one. I'm sure he'll get really scared,' suggested Jessie in her all-knowing tone of voice.

'Jessie, my name is Francesca.'

'Yes, but I think that Franjessica is a better name for you. You could change it to be part of me!'

During the summers from 1990 until 1993 as music filled the air of Paris, Jessie crammed her days with as many delights as she could. EuroDisney was a treasure chest of magic, but it was at the Lip Fountain where Jessie danced and giggled more than other places.

As Jessie waved goodbye to the Eiffel Tower, none of the family knew that they would not be returning to the Orion, nor be part of the 1994 opera season. ❧

Holiday in Paris

Once upon a time there lived two very poor mice.
There mother had left them to live for them selves
when they were very young.
So they had to steel things to eat which was a criminal
but it wasn't there fault.

From Jessie's journal

chapter Ten
JESSIE AND SUSIE

Jessie didn't mean to drop it. The fairy story book skated down ten stairs, hit a wall, made a sharp traverse to the left and slipped under the door, out of reach, into the basement flat. Unexpected things seemed to happen when she and Susie played together, and today was another adventure. They giggled as they watched the book take off at lightning speed with a life of its own. They shrieked as the glossy cover slammed into the wall, and they stared open mouthed as it disappeared out of sight. How could the book have slipped through the narrow gap?

The day had begun with the two friends playing their favourite game of school register. As usual, Jessie was the teacher, Mrs Parkes. She tried to make her voice sound just like her, and stood up straight, holding the register high. After each name, she looked up waiting for a response. Always Susie took the role of the various pupils. When 'teacher' had ticked off the last name, she picked up her fairy story book and said, 'You can't catch me.' They started chasing each other around the second floor and then down the stairs giggling all the time. That's when the accident happened. The book leapt out of Jessie's hand, did a ski jump over the handrail and raced at downhill speed into the rented flat below.

'Oh no!' Susie squeaked in her high-pitched voice. Covering her mouth with her hand, she knocked off her glasses. 'Oh no', she squeaked again standing in the hallway, looking anxiously toward the music room and then into the kitchen. What if Jessie's mother, who was practising her clarinet in the music room, heard them? Jessie stood grinning at the top of the stairs, fascinated by the disappearing act of the book. Turning to face Susie, she said in her low voice, imitating a detective, 'We must get my book.'

'But you can't. Your mum won't allow it. Somebody lives down there. No, Jessie, we must *not* get the book. It can wait. I'm afraid we'll get caught.' Susie sounded like a mechanical toy that needed to be oiled.

'How can we read a fairy story if we don't have a book? I know where the key to Sarah and Paul's flat is kept. Let's get it and go down,' Jessie insisted.

Jessie moved toward the keys that she knew were hanging behind the kitchen door. She walked lightly rather than with her usual heavy steps and noisy bounces. 'How could someone so thin be so noisy?' her grandmother had often asked. Jessie, enjoying the challenge, seemed to hear some inner prompting telling her to 'do it'. Reaching for the key on the hook, she hesitated. A different voice within her was saying, 'Don't'. Should she obey the rules of her parents or should she be adventurous and take a risk? What would be her excuse if she was caught? Turning to look at Susie, she saw her friend hiding her face in her lap as she sat on the stairs leading to the first floor. Fearful Susie lacked Jessie's urge to be adventurous, but faithful Susie would usually follow Jessie's decisions. Jessie heard her friend mumbling, 'Don't do it, Jessie. Your Mum will be angry.'

Susie and Jessie first met when they started at Park Grove playgroup at

susie and Jessie

age three. Instantly they became best friends in and out of school. Susie's father, named them 'The Gigglers,' which is what they did most of the time. They argued often as well. Jessie's mother had once said to Susie, 'Jessica will look after you.' How could she possibly be looked after by someone as daring as Jessie? When they played school register, Susie naturally fell into a responsive role. She was too shy to be the teacher.

One time at Park Grove after lunch when they were at school, the two friends were chatting in the playground. 'I'm going to read my favourite book *Little Bear* for the school assembly,' said Susie, surprising Jessie by being the first to make a suggestion. Jessie immediately came back with, 'I'm going to read that story too.'

'Jessie, no, we can't have the same story.'

'Yes we can.' Annoyed with her friend, Susie marched out of sight to a corner where she couldn't see her. Now she understood how Hannah felt when she got upset with her obstinate younger sister. Jessie stayed firmly in her place. Neither of them said a word. Only the shuffling of their feet broke the silence.

A long time passed. Then Susie heard a giggle from Jessie's corner. She couldn't help herself, she had to giggle too. The hurt and anger left both of them with that low, husky giggle. Bouncing out of their corners simultaneously, they grabbed hold of each other's hands and skipped out to the playground, laughing with released energy.

Now, with the book-in-the-basement-problem, Susie once again wanted to hide from her friend. Her curled-up body and hidden face shook with anxiety. Being looked after by Jessie was risky and scary. Jessie, sensing her friend's distress, came over and put her arms around her. 'I don't have to go down there. We can wait,' she said in a comforting voice.'

Susie's breath returned to her. 'We can, Jessie. It is better to wait. We can play something else. Should we do the school register again?' She paused to take another deep breath. 'Even better, you told me that you would teach me how to hold the bow for your violin.'

'Ok. We can do that.' Jessie paused and waited a dramatic minute before saying, 'But, look, I've got the key to the basement flat. If we were really quick and quiet, we could do it without anyone knowing. '

'But you said we could wait.'

They sat on the stairs together in silence thinking their own thoughts. Susie knew that getting the book *now* was fixed in her friend's mind. She longed to go home and leave Jessie to her own schemes. But she couldn't go home because she had to wait for her mum to pick her up.

'Susie, I'm going. Come with me. We'll be quick.'

'No, Jessie. You must wait until Paul and Sarah come home. They'll give you your book.'

'I've got a great story to read to you. It's a good one. You'll like it a lot.'

Jessie took Susie's hand and pulled her to her feet.

At the bottom of the stairs, Jessie turned the key in the lock. She grinned at Susie.

'Hurry up Jessie, I'm scared to death.'

Jessie, quick as lightning, picked up the book, locked the door and the two flew up the stairs to Jessie's bedroom on the second floor. Shutting the door, they fell on the bed safe from being found out with their hearts pounding and their breath puffing. After several minutes, Susie, looking up at Jessie's posters of horses to calm herself, asked cautiously,' Are you going to tell your mum? '

'Of course not,' said Jessie.

'But what if she finds out?

'She won't unless you tell her. Do you remember when we were cleaning the glass tank at school and the stick insects escaped?' Jessie began to laugh. 'Nobody found out then.'

'I was so scared. We didn't tell Mrs Telford did we?'

'Of course not. Do you want to play school register again? I'll read out the names of everyone in our class and you tick them off.' Jessie took on the tone of their teacher, Mrs Parkes, once again.

'I'd rather you teach me how to play the violin. You promised.'

Just as Jessie stood to go downstairs to the music room, the doorbell rang. 'Susie, your mother is here,' called Lesley up the stairs. 'It's time for you to go home.' ∞

Every day passes
And I still need glasses
Why should it be
That it has to be me.

From Jessie's poem 'Glasses' February 1994

Chapter Eleven
THE MONEYBOX

'No more treatments!' Jessie's parents decided to tell the consultant at St James's University Hospital Children's Day Unit on 2 April 1994. Waiting to communicate this message to him was tiring. 'Why doesn't he come, mummy? It's getting boring sitting here.'

Lesley tried to occupy her daughter with other things to think about, but today Jessie didn't feel up to it. Then she remembered her grandparents who were driving all the way up from Cornwall to see her. In a few days her grandfather would celebrate his 70th birthday. 'We've got to get Grampi a present. Hannah, take Daddy to the shops and buy a Swiss Army Knife. I'll pay you back when we get home.'

'And why would my father want a Swiss Army Knife?' asked Alan. 'I've never known him to even have a penknife.'

'Let's go and find one, anyway. If Jessie thinks Grampi needs one, then he must have it,' added Hannah grabbing her father's hand. She, too, was getting tired of waiting. 'You said that you would pay us back Jessie. Are you sure that you know where the key to your moneybox is?'

Don't forget to get some shiny gift wrap paper too,' added Jessie as her sister and father walked out of the waiting room.

Instead of thinking about the tiresome waiting, Jessie started talking about gifts she had bought. 'Remember when I was a little girl and I bought Grampi a green Christmas Tree candle? Do you remember that Mummy? And he kept it and never lit it, but it turned turquoise. He shouldn't have left it in the sun. Granny found a vase that her mummy had given her. It was turquoise too. She put the candle and the vase with flowers in it on her dining room table. That vase must be very old.'

From an early age, Jessie had been developing into a natural businesswoman. She was just the opposite of Hannah, who couldn't save tuppence, as her father would say about her. Jessie thought of ways to make money and to make sure she kept it safe. Both sisters enjoyed playing 'shop' when they were pre-school age, but their aims were different. One day Jessie suggested, 'Let's invite Kate and May over to buy things from our shop. We could make some money.'

When their friends arrived, Kate saw a KitKat on the pretend-shop counter. 'I'll buy the KitKat, please.' At that moment, Hannah reached for the chocolate biscuit, tore back the wrapper and popped it into her mouth. Shocked and disappointed, Kate and May decided that they didn't want to play this game any longer. Jessie protested too. 'Hannah, that's not fair. We could have made some money selling that.'

Her money saving instincts first came alive when she was five years old and her grandfather sent her a five-pound note for Christmas. From that moment, she became a banker. She kept coins and notes locked in her moneybox, and only she knew where she kept the key. However, when writing a thank you note to Grampi to tell him that she had put his gift in her money box, she spotted one spelling error. Being the perfectionist that she was, she crumpled up the paper and asked Lesley for another piece of stationery. 'I can't have any mistakes on my thank you notes. It's not right.'

As her illness progressed and Jessie no longer attended classes at Park Grove School, she converted an area of the kitchen into a jewellery manufacturing corner. 'Buy me some things from Craft Basics, Mummy. I can make jewellery to sell to my friends. I might give some away as presents.'

Whenever anyone came to visit, the selection of jewellery with the prices clearly marked on each item were on view. Jessie kept her moneybox and receipt book within easy reach. Granny Joyce has a receipt for £4.45, which declares in Jessie's neat handwriting that she had purchased a pair of earrings. 'Handmade by Jessie, and not exactly a

March 25th: Went to Oma's
for tea. We had Soup, chicken,
potatos, cabbage and Leeks.
March 26th: Went to Gilly-
gate to look at the new Shoe
Shop Bought some things
for the Jessie Fund shop
from Craft Basics. I had
naughty. CHEESE and
Potato pie.

..................25./3/19   No...2.........

**Received
from**...Joyce...George.....................
The sum of...Four...pounds...forty...-
......five....pence.........................

Cheque		
Cash	4	45
Discount		

Jessica George.....

WITH   THANKS

cheap pair,' Joyce said, as she still cherishes both the receipt and the earrings.

Words as well as money fascinated Jessie. She liked to play with them. Once she wrote in her notebook, 'Thank you god for Autumn. Are men.' When she could no longer play her violin or the piano, she decided to write poetry. 'I'll write enough poems to put in a book. Then I can sell them and get more money for my treatment,' suggested Jessie, always thinking up new ideas for solving problems. This commercial poetry enterprise sprang into being before the 'no more treatments' decision. Friends and family members had already begun to contribute to a 'tumour treatment fund'. Jessie, included in all of the family discussions during her illness, decided on the name.

'We will call it Jessie's Fund,' she proclaimed with absolute certainty.

The treatment never happened.

Jessie's Fund continues. ∞

...remind me of the rising sun...

Poems by Jessica George

Jessie's poetry book posthumusly published in 1994 for the tenth anniversary of Jessica's birth on 22nd October.

The Evening Sun

Slowly, slowly my cough runs away,
Slowly, slowly, each and every day.

From Jessie's poem 'Cough', 23 April 1994, her last poem

chapter Twelve
A LAST APPLAUSE

As the last note of Beethoven's *Symphony Number 5* sounded loud and clear, Jessie sprang to her feet and began to clap. Her face radiated pride, her smile delight, as her eyes focused on the wind section. Watching her mother play her clarinet filled her with warm feelings of love. Once she knew that Lesley had seen her, she turned toward her father to catch his eye. He caught sight of her and grinned as he lowered his viola. Now all she had to do was to wait for them to finish taking bows. Then she would race onto the stage.

Last night she had attended a concert as well. For that evening she enjoyed Beethoven's *Piano Concerto Number 5, The Emperor*. Tonight was a live recording of the *Fifth Symphony* by the John Eliot Gardiner Orchestra at the Palau de la Musica in the centre of Barcelona. Sitting in the front row, as close as she could to the orchestra, Jessie could watch all her friends play their instruments. She never tired of hearing them, especially her parents, perform.

Coming to Barcelona with Lesley, Alan, Lucy and her childminder proved a bit more demanding and complicated with Blob, her tumour. The journey became possible since Blob was taking a break from fast growth. The hospital labelled it 'in remission'. Jessie thought it was great to have Anna Tilbrook, a music student and friend at the University of York, come to be with her. They could explore the enchanted city of

Barcelona while her parents were busy rehearsing. Jessie, being the first in the entire concert hall to stand and applaud, smiled her happy smile at Anna, who stood to clap for the performance as well.

When the applause had finally ended, Jessie pointed to the bust of Beethoven, a prominent figure high up in the concert hall, 'Look, Anna, I think Beethoven is pleased with hearing his *Fifth Symphony* being played here in this magical garden. He couldn't be deaf in this place.'

'How is it a garden, Jessie?' asked Anna.

'Look at the bright coloured tiles all over the hall. There are flowers curling up the columns. It's like an outside garden that has been brought inside. I love this place. It is growing with life.' Jessie continued

pointing at the colourful tiles all around the Palau de la Musica. For a moment, Anna thought that Jessie's own colourful personality and desire to blossom in life was encircling the flower tiled columns, becoming one with her surroundings.

'Let's go find Lucy and Mummy and Daddy, Anna. I'm getting tired now.'

Only by taking a self-catering flat in Barcelona,

could Lesley keep to the special diet she had for Jessie, one that she hoped would counteract the growth of Blob. She lovingly bought organic produce and tried to prepare tasty meals, all without salt and oil. On one evening, Lesley announced that she was making a barley stew. As they all sat down to the table, Lesley was rewarded with Anna saying, 'I hope you don't mind if I don't eat this. I can't do without salt or seasonings on this stew.'

Anna Tilbrook, Jessie, Alan and Lesley

Jessie's response didn't offer any solution for her friend, Anna. 'No salt for me; no salt for anyone.'

In order for Anna's palate to survive, she must have found somewhere to snack during the day as she was escorting Jessie around Barcelona. After the day at the zoo, they strolled through *Las Ramblas* when suddenly Anna started to walk much faster, insisting that they get back to the flat. Something she had eaten had made her ill. Once in the flat, she lay down and began groaning in pain. 'Don't you worry, Anna, I'll take care of you,' said Jessie, becoming an instant nurse and reversing their roles. She found a flannel and dipped it in cold water. 'I'll put this over your forehead to make you feel better. You stay still for a while and you'll be better.'

With the concerts completed and Anna recovered from her food poisoning, Jessie and her company of family and friends left the colourful city of Barcelona. 'I wish that I could see Beethoven smile,' she said, waving goodbye to the Palau de la Musica for the last time.

Later in the year during the Proms at the Royal Albert Hall, Gardiner's orchestra once again performed Beethoven's *Fifth Symphony*. Jessie never knew of this live recording, nor had the pleasure of reading the information on the CD:

> THE RECORDING OF THIS SYMPHONY IS
> DEDICATED TO THE MEMORY OF JESSICA GEORGE,
> DAUGHTER OF ALAN GEORGE AND LESLEY
> SCHATZBERGER. ∝

A Last Applause

When the sun rises on the pretty sea,
Lots of people hope the day will be good.

From Jessie's poem 'Sunrise'

Chapter Thirteen
GOING TO CHURCH

'Did you see that Mummy? May's uncle is pushing her. He's forcing her to kneel in front of him. Kate is already down,' said Jessie in her hushed but throaty voice. Whispering wasn't easy for her.

'Be quiet, Jessie. You shouldn't talk in church,' corrected Lesley, afraid that others might hear.

Jessie didn't understand anything about the Church of England or any church services. She was here because her lifelong friends, who lived at Number 16, had invited her. Spring warmth filled the air this April 1994, and Jessie didn't want to miss celebrations of any kind since she was feeling better. Today was extra special for Kate and May since their father's brother, Uncle David, had just been made a bishop. He had asked to confirm them.

As soon as the organ began to play at the end of the service, Jessie leapt out of her pew to find Kate and May, who had taken a place near the door. They were standing next to their bishop-uncle. Jessie stood waiting for her chance to get close to them. She watched as each person leaving the church shook hands with her friends, honouring what they had done, and then stopped to say polite things to the bishop. Finally seeing her chance, she squeezed ahead to get alongside May. The question she had to ask her couldn't wait any longer. 'He pushed you

Left to right: May, Jessie, Hannah, and Kate a few years before Kate and May's confirmations

didn't he? I saw it!'

Bending down to whisper to her younger friend, May, feeling embarrassed, assured Jessie, 'Yes, he did. I didn't know what to do. When I saw the others standing, I thought that I should keep standing. But then Kate was kneeling on the other side of me. I got confused. Should I stand or should I kneel? My heart was beating so badly. I went red in the face. Did you see?'

'I saw it and thought your uncle was being a bit forceful. He pushed you hard on the head. Did he hurt you?

'I didn't want anyone to see me. Did I look silly?' asked May.

'No. I don't think anyone else noticed. My mummy didn't see the push. What was it like being confirmed?'

'I don't know yet. I just hope that my Uncle David won't be angry with me for making a mess of his very first confirmation service,' said May as she turned away from Jessie to accept the greeting of more of the congregation.

'You'll be fine. At least you are confirmed, whatever that means. See you later,' said Jessie and she looked for her mother to walk back to Number 10.

Strolling up their street hand in hand, Jessie started to say aloud the names of friends that she had known all her life. 'Number 16, May and Kate and Sara and Martin; Number 11 with Daniel and Matthew and Bethany and Peter and Yvonne. You remember, Mummy, that Matthew tried to organize the six of us into a gang? I don't think that he even knew what a gang was. We just had fun playing together. We could have had our own orchestra on our street, couldn't we? We all play an instrument or sing. What is a gang?'

Climbing up the stairs into Number 10, Jessie turned to Lesley. 'I'm glad that you went with me to see May and Kate. It was a nice service even though I didn't know any of the songs nor why the bishop did what he did. St Olave's is a warm church, Mummy. Even though we are not Christians, I like to go in there. It is warm.'

'What do you mean by warm, Jessica? asked Lesley.

'Warm means I feel something good there. Something that makes me feel like I want to be there. Warm is calm. Do you remember when you took me to that other church in the City Centre? I didn't feel warm there. I'd call that a cold church. That's all I mean. I'm going to write a poem for my friends confirmation, even though I still don't know what it means.' ℭℛ

Going to Church

To May

In your confirmation
you were shy
They pushed you down
and you tried to stay high
You said your words nice and clear.
Were you in a lot of fear?

To Kate

Well done in your confirmation,
You were with a relation
You looked ever-so nice
like sugar and spice
it's enough to
start a good conversation.

April 29: At four o'clock we went to Martin House,
to stay for a couple of nights.
April 30th: I had my first bath. It was nice. For lunch we had
cauliflower cheese, carrots and meat.

From Jessie's journal

Chapter Fourteen
A CAKE CELEBRATION

The design of the kitchen at Martin House Children's Hospice said 'children are welcome here.' It had no doors to lock anyone out. Jessie thought that this was a great place to be. Children able to stand leaned on the counter and watched whatever was going on. For those wanting to try their hand at cooking, all the bowls and pans, cutlery and mixing spoons were within their reach.

Ever since she was three years old, Jessie had learned the basics of baking. She started in Oma's kitchen learning to sift flour, beat eggs, measure the sugar and scrape the bowl. Naturally, she licked the spoon while Oma turned her back to set the oven temperature.

When Jessie went to Martin House she met Robin, who welcomed her into his domain. 'Here is where we keep snacks and drinks. If you want to plan a meal, I am glad to help,' he would say to introduce newcomers to his kitchen. Within a few days of being at the hospice, Robin and Ginny, her main carer, appreciated that this nine year old generally knew what she wanted. Even though she had lost her ability to speak, Jessie's presence and personality continued to come through loud and clear. They were not surprised when she wheeled up to the kitchen to declare that she wanted to bake a cake and some fairy cakes.

On her homemade alphabet board, she pointed to the letters, 'Make cake and fairy cakes.'

'Great idea, Jessie. What kind of cake would you like? Fruit cake or sponge cake?'

Quickly she spelled out, 'Sponge, treacle. I'll help you.'

'Who do you want the cake and fairy cakes for?' asked the smiling cook as he reached for the flour from one of the cupboards.

'For friends & family—visitors.' She pointed to the round table nearby and to the picture board on the wall behind it. At the top of the board was an overarching bright rainbow. Photographs of children who had known the loving care of Martin House were attached under the rainbow. 'Here we'll have my cake and fairy cakes. I'll call it my Getting Better cake.'

'How can we help to make this getting better in May a happy celebration?' asked Ginny. allowing Jessie to remain in charge. 'We do have flowers in the garden to pick and there are plenty of candles around.'

The same kind of cooperative atmosphere had not been present six months earlier in her grandmother's kitchen. Jessie's mood had swung to a different level on that winter day in 1993. Each December, Oma invited Hannah and Jessie to bake and decorate a ginger-bread house in their preparations for Christmas. On this particular day, the baking part progressed well with the girls happily measuring and mixing. Just before the ginger-bread house was to come out of the oven, Jessie suddenly shifted from being peaceful and cooperative to being demanding, untraditional and impractical. Her suggestion was quickly rejected by both Oma and Hannah.

'All-Sorts, Brazil nuts, and cinnamon sticks would completely spoil our ginger bread house. It doesn't fit Christmas. Be sensible, Gucki. I bought Smarties for you to decorate the house with. We always used Smarties. Why are you spoiling it now? You and Hannah can make any design you like with Smarties. I don't know where you found those All-Sorts, but put your liquorice away,' insisted Oma.

Jessie stamped her feet, raised her deep, husky voice, and restated her demands. 'This is what **I** want.' Hannah grabbed hold of Oma's apron to support her in trying to hush her nine-year-old sister.

Nothing worked. Jessie only got louder and more aggressive. Finally, Oma couldn't take anymore. The next time that Jessie increased her decibels and stamped more fiercely than before, Oma grabbed her thin, lithe body from behind and dragged her granddaughter out of the kitchen firmly closing the door behind. 'Jessica, you stay out of the kitchen until you calm down. If you can't be cooperative, then you are not welcome in my kitchen,' said Oma in her most definite voice. Whenever she became angry, her Viennese accent became more pronounced. Jessie had learned over the years that this voice of Oma's meant business, but on this occasion she continued her uncontrolled behaviour. The hollering and pounding of her feet on the floor got louder. Eventually she stomped out all the demands she had made. Then Jessie opened the door and said sheepishly, 'I put my All-Sorts away. Where are the Smarties? I'll help Hannah.'

Just over five months later, Jessie, invaded by Blob, approached baking in a different manner in the kitchen at Martin House. Standing by the counter near Robin as he was beating the eggs, Jessie silently watched in appreciation. She was only half listening to Robin who chatted as he stirred the mixture with a big spoon. Today her mind was on offering pieces of her cake to her family and giving fairy cakes to her visiting friends. Wanting to be helpful, she tried to reach for a smaller spoon to stir with, but instead she knocked against the salt cellar by mistake. 'Thanks, Jessie, just a little salt goes a long way—like an act of kindness. Your friends are going to love these.'

As the cake tins and bun trays disappeared into the hot oven, Jessie's care assistant announced rest time. 'Come back after a while and we'll ice the cake,' called Robin as Ginny wheeled Jessie away.

On her alphabet board, she wrote, 'Add sweets. I choose.'

Jessie's visitors arrived in time for afternoon tea. Jessie motioned them to sit around the table under the rainbow display. She pointed to the dozens of photos of children who had found their place at Martin House. 'I need my photo there.' Then Jessie indicated who should have a piece of cake and who should have a fairy cake. Making decisions had always come easily for her.

For this 'getting better' occasion, Jessie pointed to her alphabet board as Lesley said aloud; 'Cake, Oma. Cake, Opa. Cake Hannah, Daddy and Mummy.' When Jessie noticed that Ginny was leaning on the counter, she motioned her to come over. 'Ginny–fairy cake.'

'Let's lift our glasses and drink to this celebration. Jessie has made a cake for us,' said Alan giving his daughter a smile while raising his glass of orange squash.

Later in the day as other friends arrived, Jessie gathered them around the same table and indicated to her mother that she should read out what she said to each one. A sense of Jessie's presence filled the room.

'This is a very special time for a very special person,' commented Ginny.

Toward the end of the day when Jessie was in her bed and Hannah and Alan were playing a computer game, another visitor arrived at a specific time selected by Jessie. The remainder of the cake and a few fairy cakes were on the side table.

'Sharon—last fairy cake. Sharon—pray,' came the request through the alphabet board. ଔ

From Jessie's journal in her mother's handwriting:
May 6th, 4.45 a.m.
PACEM

Jessie's Story

Memorial Poem

An excerpt from a poem composed for the commemoration of Jessie's 10th birthday, 22nd October, 1994

Christ, where were you?

Just a tiny miracle was all

we asked, and you ignored our prayer –

or so it seems – (Dear God,

it isn't easy playing priest –

such questions may be childish

but they are sincere.

Oh, prove them wrong, who are so sure

you don't exist – grant us some doubt

in death, some faith in life – even now

a sense of something strong, stable as love

certain as our presence here.   *Amen).*

Desmond Heath

Chapter Fifteen
BIG SISTER HANNAH'S MEMORIES

On the day of Jessie's funeral, just three days after she died, Hannah sat as far back as she could in the chapel of Martin House Children's Hospice. Her gaze was fixed on the bright brass rings adorning the coffin. 'Jessie would have loved these brass rings,' was the one positive thought that sustained her.

She had nothing hopeful to hold on to after Lesley and Alan had told her that they planned to take Jessie to a children's hospice for respite care. Hannah couldn't believe that they were serious. 'That's not right. We should keep her at home with us.' For her parents to even think of such a plan was anathema to her. The day before Jessie went to stay at the hospice, Alan drove Hannah the ten miles to Boston Spa so that she could see for herself what the hospice was like. Walking into the room reserved for Jessie, she had an immediate change of heart. The carers had decorated the room with a 'Welcome Jessie' banner, and she knew that 'It was a good place. It would be OK.'

At Martin House, Jessie wasn't the only one cared for. Carol, one of the care assistants, took Hannah under her wing. Carol, who seemed to sense what was happening to Hannah, invited her to go outside of the hospice to help her feed the geese in a nearby pond. As she gradually began to feel secure and comfortable, she found it easier to express how she felt about Jessie's need for constant care and attention. Only

Sisters together, ages 5 and 3

realizing it years later, Hannah had closed in on herself for the last six months and hadn't talked about her feelings, especially not with her parents. At Martin House, however, she was offered friendship by someone giving her special attention so that she began to feel life coming back to her.

Then on 6th May Jessie died. Hannah refused to go anywhere near the special room where Jessie lay. On the day before the funeral as she and Carol walked down the hall chatting, Carol stopped in front of the door of that special room. Her carer looked at Hannah thoughtfully and asked if she could open the door just a little. In one quick second, Hannah caught sight of her sister. Not being able to take another look, she slumped down in a heap on the floor just outside the door.

A decade passed before Hannah's memories of her sister found words to share with others, especially with Lesley and Alan. With 'time as the healer' Hannah came to acknowledge how much she admired the way Jessie had handled her illness. 'Jessie would get frustrated and angry. She would talk to Blob, the tumour, about growing so big and so fast.' When Jessie could no longer sit up, her frustration intensified. Hannah recalled that she spoke in sharp tones to Blob with energy from her anger. On more than one occasion, she told Blob that she would fight it until it got smaller and smaller. But she never resorted to self-pity. Hannah said, 'I never heard her say, "Why me?"'

There had never been a question between them about Hannah being the 'big sister'. Even though Jessie had an assertive personality and often took the lead, Hannah kept her position as the older one of the two. When Hannah got angry, she would begin by shouting loudly and then run off to be on her own. Jessie, on the other hand, moved to a particular corner in the kitchen and buried her face. She wanted the world to see her displeasure and wounded feelings. 'She was powerful with her sulks,' recalled Hannah.

Looking back to the years when they were young and needed to be cared for by *au pairs* while their parents were away working, Hannah, somewhat ashamedly, recalled the alliances that she and Jessie had formed. 'Without any preconceived plans, Jessie and I joined forces to give some of the *au pairs* a difficult time. We bullied our last *au pair*, Marie, and made her life miserable. I imagine that she wished she had never come to care for us.' Their established pattern came into being as soon as their parents gave them a last hug and kiss and said good bye.

Hannah would start to worry herself sick. Jessie also hated to see her parents leave, but she would quickly turn her attention to caring for her older sister. She became Hannah's 'comforter'. She would put her arms around her and say, "It's OK Hannah. It'll be all right.' But reverse roles weren't always possible. 'She wouldn't let me console her when she was upset. The time Jessie got a "second best" for Grade 2 Violin, I tried to comfort her. She refused my care and pushed me away, I began to feel guilty that I had received the top mark for Grade 3 Flute!'

Hannah was the first to acknowledge that Jessie was the more natural musician, but she recalled how Jessie disliked practising scales and resented prescribed pieces of music. 'She hated it when Mum would practise with her. She did not like being told what to do, especially by Mum. In one of her stubborn frames of mind, she would scowl and say "no". She insisted on being right and she refused to back down.' Then this older sister commented about her younger brother, 'Jacob screws up his face in exactly the same way.'

Both girls loved to dress up, especially for special occasions. Hannah recalled that Jessie got hand-me-down clothes from her. On one glorious occasion, however, in Sienna, Italy, their grandparents took the girls shopping. For this treat they could chose a new tee shirt and skirt. Hannah took a circular red skirt with white flowers on it and began to twirl around. To her surprise, Jessie decided on the same red skirt, with a slight difference. It had spots instead of flowers. They both grabbed for the same red tee shirts at the same time. 'Generally, she refused to be just like me. She had a mind of her own,' reflected Hannah.

For Hannah, one of the strongest memories that has stuck with her is the desire both of them had for a brother or sister. 'We pestered Mummy often for a baby.' While Jessie never got to enjoy a little brother, Hannah observed that Jacob, born after Jessie's death, has her 'stubborn frown' and her 'front teeth with a gap between them. He plays her violin and writes stories just like Jessie.'

'I miss her a lot, but in a funny way I feel like she is always with me, a part of me in my memories.' ⚬

chapter sixteen
JACOB WANTS TO BE FAMOUS*

The clock rang out ten chimes and Jacob George heard his mother
say that it was time for him to go upstairs and get ready for bed. His
grandfather, Opa, sitting at the kitchen table, thought that an eight-
and-a-half year old boy should be in bed. His grandmother, Oma,
nodded in agreement while reading a draft of one of Jessie's stories
written by the family friend.

Ignoring the bedtime noises, the parental looks and nods, Jacob
removed a few pages of the story from his grandmother's hand and
started reading as he sat slouching on the kitchen settee. Almost under
his breath, but just loud enough to be heard by the others in the
room, he said, 'I want to be famous.' Several minutes passed as Jacob
continued reading while biting into his late night sandwich of raspberry
jam spread between two slices of white bread. Across the room his
mother was opening a bottle of Italian Red for her parents and friend.
As the cork was released from the bottle, she said once again to her son,
'Jacob it is time for you to get ready for bed. It is now just after ten
o'clock.'

'I want to be famous.' The words slipped quietly into the room for the
second time. What brought this idea into Jacob's thinking on this April

*I wrote this for Jacob the day after the performance

- 95 -

night in 2004? Along with the others, he had attended a premiere student musical of O. Henry's short story, 'The Gift of the Magi', at the Sir Jack Lyons Concert Hall at York University. Afterwards he watched while students dropped coins into a bucket in aid of Jessie's Fund. If Jacob were famous, would his name be on the musical programme? Would there be a bucket for people to drop money into just for him? Maybe this was the reason that Jacob wanted to be famous, so that his name would be mentioned in theatres, or on television, or in musical productions. Tonight it wasn't his name that was being mentioned in the concert hall nor around the kitchen table; it was Jessie's.

When Jessie was alive, she wasn't exactly a famous star. In fact, she was similar to Jacob in appearance, mood, and creativity. However, before she died, Jessie gave her name to a fund which would become a charity known throughout the UK. Jacob never knew his sister in person since

he was born nineteen months after her death, but he most definitely
knew her presence. From the kitchen settee where he was half sitting,
half lying down, he could see a picture of Jessie on the mantelpiece
and another one hanging on the wall. Each time he walked upstairs
to his bedroom, he would pass more pictures of Jessie. In the office on
the first floor, he could see stacks of newsletters with the large print
on the front of them proclaiming 'Jessie's Fund' –the charity he knew
well for giving access to music therapy to children in hospices. Jessie's
books, Jessie's violin, Jessie's toys were constant reminders of his sister's
presence. Jessie's pervasive presence seemed to blind Jacob from seeing
how many of his own pictures were visible on walls. He failed to see his
own numerous toys and electronic gadgets scattered around the house.
During these blinkered times, he lost track of how much his family
expressed their love and admiration for him.

Just before eight o'clock that evening, his family and friend had arrived
at the concert hall so that his mother could make sure that the Jessie's
Fund display was set up properly. Before pushing through the door,
Jacob noticed on the right a large rock placed among a collection of
smaller pebbles. On impulse, he bent to touch the heavy rock. 'I can
lift this,' he bragged, in spite of his grandmother's caution. The rock
had no special features; it was simply a heavy, large rock. Once Jacob
had spotted it, the challenge was on. It was only after the performance,
when his mother was politely speaking to students inquiring about
Jessie's Fund, that restless Jacob raced down the stairs and pushed his
way out of the door. In the dark, he once again found his large rock and
bending down, he strained to lift it above his head. Successful, he put it
down. That was that. He bounded back up the stairs. Could it be that

he wanted to be famous as a weight-lifter?

Back at home after devouring the sandwich, he fell into his usual pattern of delaying going to bed at a designated time. Addressing his friend who was encouraging him to develop his writing, he said, 'I've got another story for the competition. Exactly 750 words.'

'What is this one about?' she asked.

'I've printed a copy off for you. Read it,' he ordered his older friend.

'I'll take it home to read and then I'll come over so that we can talk about it,' she replied. 'This makes two stories you have for the *Writer's News Competition* for 9-14 year olds. Thank goodness you will be nine in time for the deadline. We'll have time to work on them.'

'I've finished already. Three, not two. "Brainy Boy" and "The Survivor" and the latest is called "The Ice Castle." I want to be famous.'

It finally dawned on his friend that Jacob had said three times,' I want to be famous'. Each time the adults in the room either didn't hear him say anything, or gave a little chuckle and said nothing. Was there a deeper desire behind the phrase? Already framed and hanging on the wall was his certificate declaring that Jacob George had received Distinction for his Grade 2 Violin Examination. Coming from a family of musicians gave him a head start in becoming well-known in the world of performing arts. Was this how he wanted to be famous?

Or, maybe Jacob would rather be famous as a writer. Take for example his imaginative story, "Brainy Boy". Written just before he turned eight, Jacob introduced a conflict between a boy with natural intelligence,

Jacob the famous . . .

Zak, and another boy, Jim, who was driven to cheat in Grade 5 maths by using a calculator. The need to be top caused Jim to take shortcuts. It was Zak who finally informed the teacher that Jim was using a calculator to get his answers. The story cleverly ended with an O. Henry type twist. When Zak was given First Prize, he felt sorry for Jim so he shared with him his winning money. They became friends.

'By the way, Jacob, what did you think of the performance tonight?' asked his friend.

'The music should have stopped when the narrator was speaking. I couldn't hear his voice very clearly because of the violin, cello, clarinet, piano… the whole band was too loud. I didn't like that,' said Jacob as he stood up reluctantly to say goodnight.

In his astute assessment of a premiere performance, Jacob may have been revealing another one of his hidden secrets. Perhaps the sounds within him of wonder, imagination, creativity and vitality were making it difficult for him to hear his own voice clearly. The eight-and-a-half year old violinist, writer, weight lifter, and late night sandwich eater had had to say it three times, 'I want to be famous.' ❦

Autumn is a time when the leaves go brown
Autumn is a time when the leaves fall down
Autumn is a time for rain
Autumn is a time to complain
Autumn is a time when all the dogs bark
Autumn is a time when it goes all dark
Autumn is a time when the puddles go splash
Autumn is a time when you're in a dash.

From Jessie's journal

Epilogue
THE END—THE BEGINNING

By Lesley Schatzberger and Alan George

'Please, please, *please* can we have another baby?' Our eight year old daughter, the little one in the family, had made the same plea to her mother before, but now that we had been to see Olivia, the tiny three-day-old sister of Jessica's friend Alice, there was an urgent yearning. 'Well, it's not absolutely out of the question, but we feel very happy with our perfect little family as it is', was Lesley's attempt at a soothing reply. In those innocent late summer days of 1993 we, her parents, were blissfully unaware of the devastating blow that would shortly strike our lives with Jessie's illness and death. Neither could we have envisaged the birth nineteen months later of the longed-for baby brother whom Jessie never knew, nor the rise of a charity that was to help children like Jessie nationwide.

Sharon Stinson came into our lives at our moment of greatest need. Having had to face the bleakest of prognoses for our lovely little girl, we were ready to explore every possible avenue for hope. We were already following a rigorously healthy diet and giving Jessie huge vitamin and mineral boosts in order to strengthen her immune system, and we were hoping to take her to New York for specialist complementary treatment unavailable in the UK. Sharon's support was of a different nature: she brought warmth and a calm, spiritual peace which Jessie loved, and all of us appreciated. I know now how hard it was for Sharon, with her

A drawing by Lucy Russell of the 'complete' George family includes both Jessica and little brother Jacob, who was born 19 months after Jessica died.

deep faith, to enter the home of strangers whom she knew followed no religious belief system and were clinging onto any straw which might help their child. The burden must have been immense, but she never showed it, and she quickly won Jessie's heart, gaining a place in her Winnie the Pooh address book under the title 'praying healer'!

But neither prayer nor medicine, conventional or complementary, could save our daughter. After Jessie died, Sharon remained with us, frequently walking the short distance between her home and ours to offer us friendship and support. She witnessed the growth of Jessie's Fund, set up with money originally intended to take Jessie to New York. We knew straight away that our memorial to Jessie would combine

Epilogue

the power of music with the needs of seriously ill children. Some eight years after Jessie died, a book about the work of Jessie's Fund[1] was in the offing, and as Sharon sat with us having a coffee one morning she said, 'So who's going to write Jessie's Story?' Without a moment's hesitation, Lesley said, 'You are'. So began Sharon's adventure of drafting, writing, rewriting, and sharing the stories about an ordinary, yet extraordinary, little girl whose character speaks so clearly from between these pages.

The adventure was not only Sharon's. We had carefully stored away those possessions of Jessie's with which we felt we couldn't part, including, of course, many of her writings and drawings. Most were in an ancient leather trunk that had belonged to a great aunt of Alan, and which we keep in our bedroom. Comforted by the proximity of these mementos, we nevertheless rarely opened the trunk: to do so required a particular frame of mind. Only Jacob would occasionally ask, which seemed to make it easier; then we would naturally and willingly take out a few precious items and talk to him about them. We have always mentioned Jessie in day-to-day conversations, so there was no sense of taboo in this exploration, but somehow the request needed to come from Jacob rather than from ourselves.

But now Sharon was asking us to look deep into our memories; and so, with some trepidation, the contents of the trunk were brought out to oil our cogs. Far from being a maudlin experience there was a joy in feeling once again the closeness of Jessie through these inanimate objects, and particularly in seeing her handwriting and reading her often witty jottings. From our revived recollections Sharon's stories began to take shape—some discarded and others extensively revised—and moments from our daughters' early childhoods sprang to the fore again.

Jessie would have been amazed to know how her life was to affect thousands of children all over the UK. Having spent the last week with her at Martin House children's hospice our eyes were opened to the possibilities of music, when used as a form of communication and expression, for children who had limited ability to speak. No children's hospices knew at that time how music therapy could help these children, so we resolved to enable them to discover for themselves how beneficial it could be.

A decade later, music is an integral part of life in a children's hospice. Jessie's Fund has provided musical instruments, given workshops, and run music-making training courses for care team members. We have established posts for music therapists in children's hospices all over the country.

Whilst Jessie's Fund continues to support children in hospices through music, we have also spread our wings further; for example to hospitals, child development centres, and schools for children with special needs. One parent, writing to us from Scotland, said,

> I have seen Anna transform over the past 7 months from a frustrated, lonely, self-harming little girl with loads of anger, and very poor self-esteem, into a much calmer and happier child who is learning to deal with her frustrations, feel better about herself, and express her feelings more appropriately.

Jessie's short life has had an impact far beyond anything we could have imagined at the beginning of her story. As our daughter she remains constantly in our hearts and thoughts, but as an inspiration she reaches far beyond the circle of family and friends whose memories have been at the core of this book. ⊲

Jessie's Fund is registered charity no. 1045731. We would be pleased to hear from you if you would like further information.

Jessie's Fund
10 Bootham Terrace
York
YO30 7DH
UK

Tel/fax: 44 (0)1904 658189
Email: info@jessiesfund.org.uk
Web: www.jessiesfund.org.uk

1. *Music Therapy in Children's Hospices – Jessie's Fund in Action,* published by Jessica Kingsley. Edited by Mercédès Pavlicevic, foreword by Victoria Wood. Available from Amazon (or direct from Jessie's Fund at £16.70, including postage and packing). ISBN 1 84310 254 4.

notes
END MATTER

Wolfi (Marc) Schatzberger, Jessie's grandfather (Opa) made a violin for her. The cover for *Jessie's Story* is graced with a photo, taken by Paul Schatzberger, of the violin that Wolfi made.

Throughout the book, the small pencil portrait at the beginning of each chapter was drawn by Susie Mészáros.

Desmond Heath wrote two poems for Jessie which were read at the concert commemorating her 10th birthday, 22 Oct, 1994 at St Olave's Church, York. One of these is quoted on page 87.

Photos not credited are those from the Georges' family album with the exception of 'The Giggles' on page 59 retrieved from a photocopy of the lost original.

Jessie's writings from the last few months of her life were taken from her *Old Bear Journal.* When she could no longer write, she dictated onto her alphabet board and Lesley wrote down the entries.

All photos used with permission.

ABOUT THE AUTHOR

Sharon Stinson was born in Los Angeles, California. After graduating with a degree in English from San Jose State University, she worked with people addicted to drugs before teaching in the USA and Brazil. In 1980, she moved to York, England, to join the staff of an Anglican Church where she trained as a counsellor and spiritual companion. After 1986 she was instrumental in developing the Acorn Listener project, writing and teaching courses in the UK and South Africa. She has always written poetry, stories and articles, but this is her first book.

Printed in the United Kingdom
by Lightning Source UK Ltd.
107247UKS00001B/112-198

9 780977 483709